Happy memories of your
1986 visit home.

I love you Jean.

Mummy.

ON
MORECAMBE
BAY

Peter Cherry

PETER CHERRY ARPS

To Ced, Olive, Chris and Jean

I would firstly like to thank the Robinsons for all the love they have shown me in the four years I have been proud to know them. Thanks also to my parents for having confidence in me in the early days and to Tant, Tony—and Michael, who changed my life in a small way—I now appreciate the beauty of horses. Finally thanks to my former English teacher Miss B. MacAlpine, for checking my original manuscript and to everyone at Minstrel , Pindar .Studio 82 MCG Graphics and Ilford Ltd.

Auch, meine liebe Oma und Trudel, vielen dank an euch beide.

PC August 1984

Designed and Published by Peter Cherry, 78 Mainwaring Drive, Wilmslow, Cheshire.

Typeset by Minstrel Publications Ltd. Sale, Cheshire.

Colour repro. by MCG Graphics Ltd., Citadel Way, Hull.

Mono repro. and platemaking by Studio 82 Ltd., Citadel Way, Hull.

Printed in England by Pindar Print Ltd. Eastfield, Scarborough.

ISBN 0 9511404 0 X

CONTENTS

AN UNUSUAL CORNER OF ENGLAND

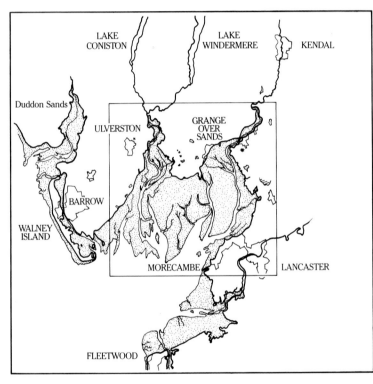

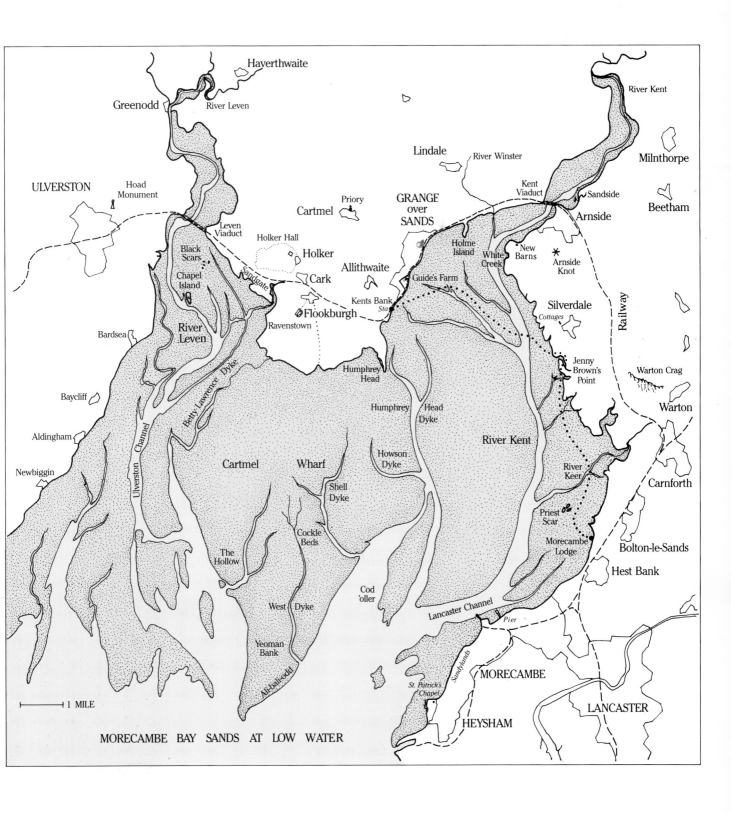

MORECAMBE BAY SANDS AT LOW WATER

1 MILE

Hayerthwaite

Greenodd

River Leven

ULVERSTON

Hoad
Monument

Leven
Viaduct

Black
Scars

Chapel
Island

Sandgate

River
Leven

Bardsea

Baycliff

Aldingham

Newbiggin

Betty Lawrence Dyke

Ulverston Channel

Cartmel

Wharf

Shell
Dyke

Cockle
Beds

The
Hollow

West Dyke

Yeoman
Bank

Ali-bali-odd

Holker Hall

Holker

Cark

Flookburgh

Ravenstown

Cartmel

Priory

Humphrey
Head

Humphrey

Howson
Dyke

Head
Dyke

Cod
'oller

Lindale

River Winster

GRANGE
over
SANDS

Allithwaite

Guide's Farm

Kents Bank
Sta

Holme
Island

White
Creek

Kent Viaduct

Sandside

Arnside

New
Barns

Arnside
Knot

Silverdale

Cottages

Jenny
Brown's
Point

River Kent

River
Keer

Priest
Scar

Morecambe
Lodge

Lancaster Channel

Pier

Sandylands

St. Patrick's
Chapel

MORECAMBE

HEYSHAM

River Kent

Milnthorpe

Beetham

Railway

Warton Crag

Warton

Carnforth

Bolton-le-Sands

Hest Bank

LANCASTER

7

SPIRIT OF THE BAY

Morecambe Bay is a special place – an exceptionally beautiful indent in the north west coastline of England. It lies at the foot of the Lake District, with the Lakeland hills as a spectacular backdrop, but is far less well known. Even less is known of the local people who follow the sands to make their living. About a dozen families on the north shore still harvest the natural richness of the bay without ever going to sea. Tractors are used at low tide to catch the famous shrimps and the whitebait, cockles and the flukes – flat fish that gave their name to the ancient fishing village of Flookburgh which lies just six miles due south of the southern tip of Lake Windermere. But the bay can equally take life away from the unwary as well as sustain it, being neither cruel nor benign. It has no conscience.

Morecambe Bay is one of the last wildernesses in England to remain unchanged by man. A sand plain of *one hundred* square miles and more, is revealed twice each day by the ebbing tide which carves the surface into subtly different reliefs each time. It is a mercurial landscape existing in two states – as sea and as sand. While infinite variations of sky and cloud endlessly tint and shade the plains of water and of land.

Almost like a living organism, the bay is itself evolving. Channels and quicksands come and go, moving themselves sometimes overnight after staying in the same lie for decades. The shore margins ebb and flow too. Marshland will be eroded in one area while new land is built up elsewhere on the bay, often in cycles spanning centuries. A thousand years from now the sand may have turned to grass, indeed, further up the estuary a grassland plain in the Lyth Valley *does* lead down to sea. Set on a hillside on the edge of this plain stands the one-time fishing village of Levens, as if curiously stranded.

Man has attempted to tame the bay in the past and failed. The remains of a lonely mile long wall recently exhumed by the sea stretches out from Silverdale shore – built over a century ago as the start of a grand land reclamation scheme but never completed. Ironically nature has by now turned this area into a salt marsh anyway. For twenty years and more, there have been plans to build a barrage across the mouth of the bay to form a vast reservoir, but thankfully none has yet gone beyond the feasibility stage, for such a scheme would destroy the uniqueness and beauty of the sands and a whole way of life would be lost forever.

In this book, I have tried to convey the spirit of the 'inner bay' as I call it, bounded by Heysham and Flookburgh, encompassing Morecambe, Hest Bank, Silverdale, Arnside, Grange-over-Sands and Kents Bank. This collection of words and pictures is an expression of my love for the place itself and also my love for the people who make their living by 'following the sands' and have allowed me to experience and record their way of life.

Winter morning at Arnside, looking towards Grange

Overleaf – The black hump of Humphrey Head, seen from White Creek

Cottages on the Silverdale Shore

The mile-long wall stretching out from Jenny Brown's Point

A Brack, a break-away in the sands, near Silverdale

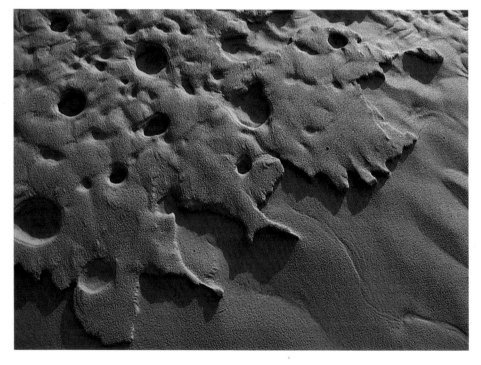

Overleaf – The snow covered Lakeland mountains, seen from Hest Bank

At the heart of the bay

Stone-cut tombs at St. Patrick's Chapel, Heysham

THE SAND PILOT

On the northern shore of Morecambe Bay nestling in Grange-over-Sands there stands a whitewashed farm house. Seen from the sands it lies at the lower right hand point of a triangular eleven-acre patch of green fields stretching up the Grange hillside with its base running parallel to the shore.

This is Guide's Farm and would have stood alone in a very wild corner of England when it was built over seven hundred years ago. It is said that Oliver Cromwell once slept there in the days when the house offered ale and an overnight stay to travellers who crossed the sands from the south shore some eight miles away. The town of Grange-over-Sands grew to surround the farm after the coming of the Furness Railway in 1857 which encircled the bay from Heysham to Barrow, crossing the Kent estuary at Arnside and the Leven estuary at Ulverston. Guide's Farm is owned by The Crown and now lived in by Cedric Robinson and his family.

Cedric was royally appointed to the ancient post of Guide to the Kent Sands in 1963 and has since guided several thousand walkers safely across the deceptively dangerous sands. Shifting quicksands come and go – changing their position sometimes overnight and Ced has to be able to recognise them. On a dozen or so occasions during the summer months he leads parties of up to several hundred people across the bay from Silverdale to Kents Bank. Just a few years ago the route was longer, starting at Morecambe Lodge and finishing at Grange, a walk of some eleven miles. But the snake of the river Kent awakened , making the channel too deep to be crossed by the old route in safety.

Cedric Robinson is a well built fisherman in his mid-fifties, with a ruddy complexion and noble Nordic features. It would be easy to believe that he could be a descendant of the Norsemen who first entered the bay a thousand years ago. Fragments of their languages are still used today by the local fisherman. Words and phrases such as 'sister theer' (look there) 'watter' (water) 'luckster' (look). Added to this a mixture and corruption of English words, makes the people of Flookburgh speak in a unique way, quite unlike Lancashire and subtly different from the Cumbrian dialects spoken a few miles around about in the Lake District. Ced's warm countenance set atop with bushy windswept hair, just starting to go grey at the edges, is distinctive and readily remembered. He makes his living by fishing the bay; receiving only a token payment for his work as guide, but is provided with Guide's Farm rent free to offset this. Coming originally from Flookburgh where his parents still live, he shares their Flookburgh dialect, but perhaps more softly.

I first met Ced in the summer of 1981, when I was twenty-two, on one of the cross bay walks from Hest Bank to Grange-over-Sands. It was a cloudless, July day and the walk was unusual in that there were only four of us on it—the Cherry family. He was already a familiar personality, having appeared on many television programmes about the bay, but at the time I was too shy to talk with him at length.

In March the following year however, I wrote to Ced explaining that I wanted to do a book on the bay, for which I already had a great affection and asking if I could take some photographs of his fishing activities, that Easter. I soon received a neatly written letter saying that he would be delighted and so I telephoned and arranged to meet him and his wife Olive at Guide's Farm the next Friday evening.

Eventually I found Guide's Farm in the uneasy darkness of the unlit end of Cart Lane and nervously tapped the brass horseshoe knocker—I had read in Cedric's book that 'Cart-er' was the old name for the sands' guide. The solid, white painted door opened and the familiar face of Cedric appeared. He smiled warmly and invited me in, saying 'Mind your head on the door.' Inside, a pair of heavy curtains served as a partition to keep in the warmth of the twelve by fifteen foot living room and a welcoming wood fire burned fiercely in a stone hearth. Ced's wife, Olive greeted me just as warmly and I took to her straight away. With fair hair, fair skin and sky blue eyes she looked remarkably fine for her years, being a decade older than Ced, and indeed a painting on the wall was testimony to her beauty in younger years. It soon became apparent too, that her genuine, soft spoken and gentle nature matched her looks.

Two, massive, dark oak beams ran the length of the living room ceiling—Ced told me he thought these were once ship's timbers—and equally substantial walls were revealed by the two foot depth of the window sill. The room was comfortably furnished with simple but solid furniture. Olive said that the round oak dining table by the window had come from Cark Station waiting room originally and after being bought, had stood out in the rain for four years before being sanded down and smartly varnished. I noticed it still bore the initials HW, carved too deeply to be removed. But most remarkable of all was the atmosphere of tranquility in Guide's Farm which seemed to almost instantly impart a feeling of peace. In a strange way I felt I had come home.

While Ced told me tales of his life as fisherman and guide, Olive plied me with mugs of tea and biscuits. Ced consulted his trusty tide table and read out a list of times and dates when he could take me along with him to fish for whitebait, flukes and cockles. At the time he was not set up for shrimping so he gave me the address of a Flookburgh fisherman whom he said was a 'decent sort' and wouldn't mind taking me out instead. Suddenly it seemed, it had become late, so I reluctantly said I must leave and thanked the couple. Feeling as if I had known them a long time, I made my exit through the theatre-like curtains.

One week later I returned to Guide's Farm. Daylight showed it to be a sturdy whitewashed building. I knocked on the familiar door and a voice inside called me in—I soon discovered that the front door is hardly ever locked. Olive was apologetic 'I'm sorry about all the mess in here but we're just doing some spring cleaning.' I said it looked fine (it really did).

'Ced'll be down in a minute'. Her husband soon appeared, smiling and asked, 'Are you ready for off?' Reluctantly I left the warmth of the fireside.

The outdoors was not inviting. Damp, cold, overcast and misty. It was already mid-afternoon and dusk would be closing in a couple of hours. I shivered, pulled on an extra pair of socks followed by green wellingtons. Ced put on his waders and yellow oilskin, climbed aboard his yellow tractor and leant forward to bring the machine to life. A precious burst of sunlight lit the yard as I opened the gate to let Ced out, then climbed awkwardly onto the machine. Hold tight Ced grinned. And we made our way the hundred yards down Cart Lane, turning right by the level crossing keeper's house to wait before the railway gates until the crossing woman emerged—a robust, lively Tyneside character called Eva. Seeing me with my camera she shouted above the noise of the engine in a mock serious manner 'How do'you want me? Left side, right side or backside!' I returned an embarrassed smile. The tractor rattled over the tracks and down the stone built ramp to the muddy shore. Wheels ploughed furrows nearly a foot deep in the sticky substance but a hundred yards further on we reached wet, but firm, sand. Ced opened up the throttle and a warm plume of diesel fumes blew in our faces. Actually welcome in the cold March air. He shouted to me above the roar of the tractor and pointed out in the direction of Silverdale to where his whitebait nets were set.

Ten minutes later the nets yielded bulging silver 'tails' which Ced undid then poured a rain of the tiny silver fish into his metal boxes. The knot was carefully retied and the net vigourously shaken to dislodge strands of seaweed. Ced strained back to set the net in line once more, and, after he attended to the remaining two nets in the same way we were soon aboard again and making for home.

The flames of the fireplace were more welcome than ever when we returned to the Farm. Olive was cooking some food and insisted that I stay for tea, and so I gratefully accepted, having a fair appetite after the afternoon's outing.

Ink-blue dusk was tinting the eight-paned living room window as we eventually sat down to eat.

Ced resets his whitebait nets. The shadow of Humphrey Head can be seen in the distance.

FLOOKBURGH SHRIMPERS

Seven o'clock on a numbingly cold early April morning in Flookburgh. I am in the back yard of a house near the village centre waiting for the shrimpers to arrive, at three hours after high water. Around the yard of this starky grey building there is an outhouse which contains fishing equipment. Next to that a stable and then a greenhouse beside which stand two old rusty, red tractors. My breath hangs in the still air and my hands and toes are gradually loosing their feeling.

Presently my solitude is ended by the arrival of Tony, locally known as 'Tant', with his two sons. Tant is a stocky man with unruly brown hair and a serious countenance. He greets me tersely. His elder son is fifteen, also called Tony but taller than his father with neatly cropped straight sandy hair. The younger boy now leads a horse out of the stables into the adjoining field. He is Michael, aged thirteen. Just above shoulder high to his brother, with straight brown hair, long handsome features and wearing a brown anorak, black waterproof overtrousers and a navy blue bobble hat without the bobble. The two Tonys soon climb into their yellow oilskins.

Few words are exchanged between the three of them, as fish boxes are loaded onto the back of the tractor together with a pair of riddles (sieves) and a short handled shovel. An implement used for cockling, called a jumbo stands on one of the two boards which have been home-fitted along either side of the tractor. Tant takes hold of a bare ended wire dangling from inside the engine and sparks this onto a terminal. The machine groans and coughs for a few seconds until a cloud of smoke emerges triumphantly from the exhaust. Michael quickly pulls a pair of working gloves out of a pocket and stretching out, carefully holds one of them open over the warming fumes. But his father impatiently shouts 'Don't be so bloody daft. It's not that cold.' Michael looks back, tight lipped and defiant.

Flookburgh Village, seen from Humphrey Head.

Tant calls at me to jump on. The contraption lurches forward and we turn into Winder Lane then right along Main Street through the village turning right again at the square to join the Mile Road. Tant drives standing–there is no seat. We travel at full speed down the dead-straight mile long road which crosses the grassy plain from village to shore–once part of the bay itself when Flookburgh was first built. Soon we slow down for a cattle grid–the gateway to the bay. Crossing the marshland margin we eventually reach the muddy end where the track dips down alarmingly into a deep dyke (channel) and the tractor strains to climb to the other side. It takes all of my grip, balance and concentration to stay onboard, but mercifully we are now on firm sand–the bay proper. A few hundred yards ahead, half a dozen long, wheeled objects can be seen.

As we approach I can make them out as trailers with nets and rope stowed ontop. Tant tells me these are always home built out of old car chassis fitted with planks and pivoted steel side arms, as he skilfully backs the tractor up to his own trailer. Tony drops in the steel coupling pin then jumps onto the relative comfort of the trailer before Tant sets off again, now flat-out into the bay. Wheels hiss on the wet sand as they trace their footprints, marking out the route. These tracks could literally become a lifeline to follow home in foggy weather, before the tide's flow floods the bay. Tant carries no compass. As it is, a morning mist shrouds the bay margins, giving the illusion that the sands stretch to infinity .

Soon another tractor and trailer comes into view behind and is evidently trying to catch up. Tant points back, shouting 'Les Butler!' and we seem a race to be the first at the shrimping grounds. A trail of strange—almost sweet—smelling sooty diesel smoke from the exhaust heralds our progress as we plough through deep channels where the water level rises to alarming heights, sometimes even above our footplate. Tant gives a rare grin. 'Don't start worrying 'till it comes up to the air intake!' he shouts above the roar of the tractor.

Time stretches out as we steam into the heart of the bay, flanked to our left by Les Butler who gradually overtakes. A veil of salt water and sand spray surrounds us. "Surely we must be there soon?" I think to myself. The journey *is* exhilarating but I can never remember feeling so thoroughly cold. Eventually, a large stretch of water emerges from the morning mist and we drive alongside for a while before Tant stops. We have reached the shrimping ground, the Ulverston channel—another name for the outflow of the River Leven—after half an hour's travelling. The trailer is uncoupled and re-attached this time by a three hundred yard long rope. Both boys swing out the rusty steel tubes from either side of the trailer to form a pair of arms, to the ends of each of which a shrimp net is tied by a much shorter rope. Each of these nets has a narrow, three yard wide, rectangular mouth with an upper bar of ash and a lower one of steel. The mesh of the net funnels back to a finer mesh tail. Both of the shrimp nets are now pulled out neatly either side of the trailer by the elder son and his father.

Tant remounts the tractor and moves off again. Pulling out the coils of rope, he enters the channel at a shallow angle to the water's edge and, driving deeper into the water until it comes just below his footplate he then steers parallel to the edge again, to keep his depth. Suddenly the trailer snatches forward from the invisible tautening of the trawl rope and trundles eerily into into the water until only the tip of the folded back towing V bar remains above the surface as a marker. The trailer does not however travel

directly behind the tractor but instead goes automatically to one side to reach the deeper water where most of the shrimps are. This is contrived by setting and locking the trailer's front wheels to always steer itself to one side, which accounts for the towing rope being about twenty or thirty degrees out of line when trawling. The steel bars along the base of the net mouth will scrape along the channel bottom, disturbing the brown shrimps in the uppermost layer of sand so that they jump up, to be swept into the tails.

Tant's first trawl takes about fifteen minutes, at a slow walking speed, then he steers the tractor onto dry sand and empties his prize from the tails. A glistening mass of brown shrimps which will turn the famous pink colour when boiled. The boys now set about helping him to riddle the shrimps, firstly with a wide mesh to get rid of crabs, seaweed, unwanted fish and general flotsam and finally with a narrower mesh to weed-out the small, immature shrimps as dictated by the Fisheries Protection Laws. In any case the women pickers wouldn't thank them for having tiny shrimps to work on. Tony suddenly picks a small silvery green fish out of his riddle and thrusts it literally under my nose declaring 'It's a *cucumber* fish!' I'm taken aback but have a sniff anyway and–yes, it smells remarkably like freshly cut cucumber!

Having riddled all the shrimps, the nets are stowed on the trailer and Tant tows it back up the channel to begin another trawl in the same direction. Meanwhile the boys spend some time cockling. Michael sets-to on the jumbo–a wooden board with handles used to bring the cockles to the surface–with grim determination and is reluctant to let me have a go. After another two trawls, Tant decides it's time to make for home, for the incoming tide will not wait. Our tracks are retraced all the way to Flookburgh as cloud begins to thin and promises to let the sun through.

Michael, Les and Tony, cockling

We arrive back in Flookburgh more than three hours after first setting off. The shaking journey was fatiguing enough in itself. But the work is not yet over, for the shrimps have to be boiled while still alive otherwise they stick in their shells which makes picking them a difficult task. The boiling is done in the outhouse in a hemispherical iron cauldron about two feet in diameter set into a brick base and heated from underneath by an oil fired burner. Tony fills this two-thirds full of water and once properly boiling pours in a box full of shrimps then puts a wooden lid on top. After a couple of minutes he lifts a pile of shrimps out with a device called a ladle—but more closely resembling a raquet with a long handle—gently blowing the steam away to see the colour of them. A silvery pink appearance would tell him if they were properly boiled. They are, so he scoops out the remainder into a basket. The boiled shrimps are tipped onto a mechanical riddle—a motorised vibrating wire mesh contraption—to remove any remaining small shrimps, then spread over wire mesh trays to dry. The vapour rising from these has a warm appetising smell, not at all fishy but difficult to describe, as we pick out and eat some of the fattest, warm shrimps which taste far better than the cold ones I'm used to. Suddenly, the steamy atmosphere flares in a shaft of clean sunlight cutting through the skylight. I feel warm again and contented, though tired. It seems like the first day of spring.

Michael has by now thoughtfully emptied out his wellingtons and removed the bobbleless hat, anorak and waterproofs in deference to the sun's warmth. He is with his favourite horse in the adjoining field. Standing with one shoulder under the animal's head he spreads his hands carefully around its nose then firmly but gently presses his face against the horse's cheek and kisses it with an intensity of passion which I hadn't seen before between man and animal. His love feels almost like a radiant energy as I look on, and after a long, last nose-squashing kiss he slowly releases the horse.

In the afternoon I met Michael again, this time in the little Flookburgh Fisherman's Co-operative Factory where he was helping his uncle Jim and his grandmother, Edna, to pot shrimps. The picked shrimps were boiled in spiced hot butter – which gave the place a wonderful aroma – then strained and one ounce portions weighed into small tubs and potted with another ounce of liquid butter, spooned in by hand. This rapidly solidified, thus 'potting' and preserving the shrimps. Agnes one of the workers there had been potting for some years as demonstrated by her deft and tranquil manner. Michael on the other hand was being rather less calm and precise but made up for this with plenty of enthusiasm.

The end product of the shrimpers labours soon piled up. Dozens of little white tubs ready for despatch to those who have a taste for the famous Morecambe Bay Shrimps.

FOLLOWING THE SANDS

Returning to Guide's Farm, in a cold mid April—back to winter it seemed—I met Ced's daughter, Jean, for the first time. She was in her late teens and had evidently inherited her mother's beauty, with echoes of her father's noble features. Jean also shared Olive's soft spoken, and in many ways, innocent nature. Ced lay, unshaven, asleep in the armchair next to the fire with a small dog in his lap while Olive thoughtfully offered me a seat closer to the fire.

Ced awoke suddenly and slowly focussed on me. 'Hello Peturr,' he purred, in his rounded Flookburgh tones and, after a yawn, 'We'll be setting off in about half an hour, at three hour's ebb.' Then, to Olive, 'How about a nice cup of tea and a biscuit first, love?', as he disappeared upstairs for a shave. Meanwhile Olive was sitting at the polished round oak table with her favourite chihuahua 'Candy', so I took the opportunity to photograph them by the soft light of the window.

After rejoining us a few minutes later, Ced sat down to tell me tales of fishermen in former days who were lost on the sand and 'never heard of or seen again' along with their 'carts, horses, and all.' Before tractors were commonly used to 'follow the sands', horses and carts were taken out instead—right up until the early sixties. The shrimpers nets were tied behind the carts and the animals had to pull these through the channels, often up to their necks in water. Many tragic stories tell of horses being drowned when mired in quicksand or when the carts started to sink, dragging the unfortunate animal with them, despite the desperate efforts of their owners to rescue them. Clearly a natural story teller, Ced then told me of how, long ago, a dead man's hand had emerged from the sands when a Flookburgh fisherman was cockling with a jumbo—used to bring the shellfish to the surface. Ced has reason enough to be wary and says that even after knowing the bay all his life he still greatly respects its ability to take life as well as sustain his livelihood. 'Surely it's possible to tell a quicksand just by looking at the texture of the surface?' I asked earnestly But Ced countered that there is no sure way of telling just from the appearance but one must also know the places where they are likely to appear, for instance round the margins where underground streams occur, and up the estuaries. But even then he claimed to require almost a sixth sense, evolved over many years, to detect them.

Quicksands are simply a mix of sand and water where the sand itself becomes like a thick liquid or a jelly, and gets progressively thinner and more dangerous when agitated, in particular when someone walks over it. A quicksand can mire its victim further when he struggles to get free then set around him 'like cement'. This is no exaggeration; attempts to drag out a person trapped to the waist by sheer force could literally tear them apart. The only effective way is to dig quickly around the victim before the sand reforms. But then, the turn of the tide becomes a second enemy. Ced told me that the best way to get out of a quicksand is to sit down or lie flat as you feel yourself sinking and crawl out without unnecessary movement; above all, without panicking. All of this imbued me with a respect for the sands which I didn't previously possess; on a sunny clear day the sands could look perfectly benign.

It was now early afternoon and Ced groaned reluctantly out of his armchair, calling 'Jean are you ready for off?' Jean appeared and protested, 'Dad do I have to go, it'll be freezing out there'. But with a sigh she pulled on her blue and white woollen hat and fingerless gloves. Ced went into the outhouse to put on the familiar yellow oilskin then gathered a bundle of pointed six foot long ash stakes and loaded them on the tractor followed by his stream nets, a long rusty pole and a couple of cockle baskets. Jean sat herself on the tail board of the tractor as Ced started it up. After closing the yard gate, I jumped onto the back of the tractor next to Jean. At the end of Cart lane we negotiated the now familiar level crossing and descended down the stone ramp to follow in the tracks made by Ced the day before. A rapier sharp wind cut across our faces as we headed in towards the heart of the bay with the twin signatures of our wheels unravelling behind us. It was overcast and the shore we left behind soon melted to a faint flat shadow in the mist, while we crossed the sand plain wilderness. In front I could see only lead–white sky meeting the seeming infinity of ribbed sand.

Minutes passed and it felt as if we were being transported into another land; to another time. There was no sound save for the diesel's roar as we traversed the ocean of sand. White spray was thrown up around us whenever we steamed through channels, shallow and deep. Still onwards. Then after more than half an hour from home a feature could just be resolved ahead; a row of thin lines etched parallel and perpendicular to the horizon. We drew nearer and turned in a neat arc to stop before them. Our destination–Ced's nets staked on ground very slightly higher than the surrounding plain.

Entangled in the fine filaments of the stream nets were flukes: flat fish with mud-brown tops and snow-white underbellies, which the last tide's ebb gathered in. Ced crouched over the net with a cockle basket under the crook of one arm. His hair swept back by the vicious wind. He deftly disentangled the first fat fluke, placing it carefully in the basket then moved along to the next. Jean helped her father, and soon all the fish were landed. Ced washed his basket-full of fish in a small pool specially dug for the purpose, splashing waves of water over them with his free hand. Suddenly, sun pierced cloud and transmuted wet sand into liquid silver for an exhilarating instant. But the heavens soon healed again.

Now the hard work began. Another two nets identical to the first were to be staked out a hundred yards apart. Firstly Ced bored holes by working a long iron rod into the stubborn sands at regular intervals, measured by taking two full paces back each time. The holes were set, not vertically, but at a slight angle so that when the ash stakes were inserted they would all slope up into the bay to withstand the ebb's thrust. Jean hammered the stakes home into these pilot holes with a wooden beater, called a mell, so that half the length of each stake was firmly implanted in the sands. After a dozen or so stakes had been set in line, Ced started to tie on his stream nets by twisting the upper and lower ropes around the wooden stakes. These ropes were to run parallel to form the mouth of the net – the lower one being set slightly off the ground to avoid catching seaweed. In between, he deftly twisted in short wood spars with his strong weather-accustomed hands to hold the mouth of the net open.

Ced told me that the sands were, remarkably, up to *seventy feet* deep in places. There must be a macabre assortment of objects lying beneath the sands – devoured by them over the centuries – I pondered. Whole stage coaches, boats wartime aircraft, carts tractors and trailers and skeletons of hundreds of the bay's victims, some a thousand years old and more, back to Roman times when people are known to have travelled over the sands as a short cut between the north and south. I shivered. Just one more to do and it'll be 'Home James', grinned Ced. Breathing into cupped hands to try and restore feeling to them, I daydreamt of the warmth at Guides Farm.

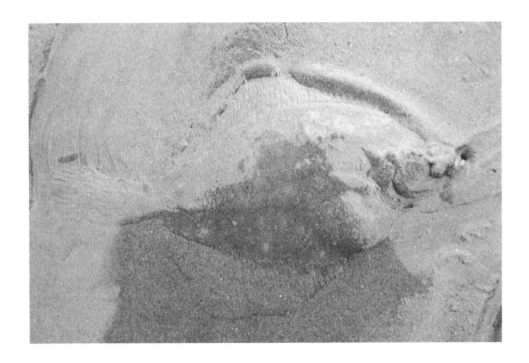

A 'Dooaking' fluke hiding itself in the sand.

I was glad when the tractor was started again and offered my hands to the diesel exhaust – a tip learned from Michael – before reboarding the tractor. The line of nets soon dissolved into silver greyness as we rattled our way homewards to the sanctuary of Guide's Farm. And a tea prepared by Olive's fair hand, with excellent cake made by Jean I must add. As my cheeks burned in the warmth and feeling returned to my (almost steaming) stockinged toes stretched before the fire, I reflected on the harshness of the life in following the sands. But Ced told me he wouldn't change his way of life for anything. I had found a family rich, not in wealth, but rather in happiness and contentment.

THE ROYAL CARRIAGE CROSSING

This much heralded event was to be the first horse drawn crossing of the Kent Sands since the days when regular stage coaches ran from Morecambe Lodge to Ulvertson well over a hundred years ago. The arrival of the Furness Railway in 1857, however, made this perilous journey unnecessary.

The event was organised by Holker Hall to mark the tenth anniversary of their horse trials. The special attraction was to be the Duke of Edinburgh who would lead the dozen or so carriages of various sizes with his four–in–hand Clevelands. Ced being guide to the Kent sands by royal charter was approached by Holker Hall and given the responsibility of guiding His Royal Highness safely across. On the day before the event, Ced walked and set out the route from Silverdale shore to Kents bank station with markers of laurel branches called brobs which he implanted in the sand. Press and television were already around about and eager to interview the guide.

The great day came, May the 30th 1985. A delicate morning mist promised to burn off to yield a summers day as I turned up at Guide's Farm. Ced had organised two tractors and trailers on which were set a line of straw bales to serve as seats for the press. By early afternoon it had become a surprisingly hot day, more usually expected in July or August, as our circus–like procession of tractors and trailers and pick–up trucks carrying an assortment of excited children from Ced and Olive's family hauled itself up the steep hill of Carter Road. The expanse of the ebbing bay revealed itself as we climbed. Turning left down Kentsford Road we soon were bumping over the railway crossing at Kents Bank Station to reach the shore just the other side. This was to be the grand finishing point. Guide ropes were being set out on the shore and a fair number of people had already gathered. We waited there and gradually the photographers and journalists arrived and scrambled aboard including most of Fleet Street, the BBC, ITV, various foreign film crews, local radio and local newspapers. As soon as all were crammed on the trailers we set off across the firm sands to our vantage point on the river Kent opposite Silverdale, where we waited, roasting in the afternoon sun. From here we hoped to get a good view of the highpoint of the event; the water crossing. The thin line of Silverdale shore cottages could just be made out in the rippling haze surrounded by a myriad tiny multicoloured specks–people, many hundreds, maybe thousands. While we waited there was a buzz of anticipation and a holiday atmosphere as the Fleet Street boys joked amongst themselves.

Ced had planned the setting off time to be seven hours ebb to give the firmest sand for crossing – three o'clock. The starting time came but no signs of movement could be seen. Twenty five minutes passed and presently the white and coloured specks appeared to shift and converge like a living organism. It stretched and focussed itself to a thin line of movement which after a few minutes could be resolved as a trail of carriages. The procession did not, however, head directly toward us but instead turned left, then right, in a meandering path to follow the safest route under Ced's pilotage. Soon the individual horses, carriages and drivers could be clearly seen. The Duke's four magnificent animals entered the water of the Kent channel first, with the remaining dozen carriages now spreading to flank left and right – a manouvre ordered by Ced. This prevented carriages from following in one anothers tracks which might effectively produce quicksand. The line of carriages ploughed the water *majestically* towards us with the smaller animals immersed almost to the neck. Two, sinister, black figures rode side by side at centre; the mounted police guard. Alarmingly, the Duke's four – in – hand thundered axle deep directly towards me it seemed, but then passed just three yards to my right. The sheer size and power of his Cleveland horses was awe inspiring. Ced with concerned concentration sat proudly next to His Royal Highness and soon the following carriages reformed behind their leader once more and strained to match his pace.

Crossing the River Kent. The Duke's four-in-hand is seen on the left

Having reached firm ground, the Duke appeared to be in no mood for a leisurely canter and briskly set course directly for Kents Bank persued by a pair of hornet–like helicopters. '. . . Couldn't hear yourself think,' the Duke reported afterwards. I swung round to photograph the historic silhouette of carriages against the painfully shining sand, but in doing so was left behind by the tractors. I ran towards the nearest trailer and thankfully the driver saw me and slowed down to let me catch up but I still had to leap onto the moving platform and bruised one leg in the process. Our driver now set full throttle and we gradually came alongside the Duke's carriage about a hundred yards to our right. We, photographers, feverishly snapped away, needing appreciable skill to hold our cameras steady while remaining on board. Very soon it seemed–actually fifteen minutes later–we were slowing down and approaching a several thousand strong crowd at Kents bank. Small boys with bicycles rode cheekily alongside to the finish.

Then the multitude engulfed the leading carriage. I jumped off the trailer and, running round to the front sporting a pink press badge and negotiating my way through the crowd, I photographed Ced next to His Royal Highness. Both were presented with an engraved crystal tankard to commemorate the event. The TV news people were eager to interview the Duke. Wasn't he worried about the treacherous quicksands? But His Royal Highness said that he had 'full faith in his guide' motioning, with a smile, towards Ced.

The triumphant procession moved off once more, parting the crowd—lined stone ramp to cross the railway tracks. On the other side Ced jumped down and bade farewell. The Duke waited a while in the welcome shade of the trees at Kents Bank, then briskly set off up the hill on route to Holker Hall just four road miles ahead.

The whole event seemed to be over so quickly—actually three quarters of an hour—but was certainly a day to be remembered. Back at Guide's Farm, Ced was received like a hero by friends and relatives. The place was more crowded than I'd ever seen it before.

We eagerly awaited the evening news reports from first ITV, then BBC. Both tried to inject drama into the report by talking of 'a race against time, tide and the treacherous quicksands' which amused us all. A race against the incoming tide it was not, and if there had been any real *danger* Ced wouldn't have allowed the crossing to go ahead. His Royal Highness may, however, have regarded any element of race as being more 'from the attentions of the media', rather than 'from the turn of the tide!'

65

A CROSS BAY WALK

Eleven o'clock at Morecambe Lodge on the southern side of the bay and a searingly hot July day. People are gathering aged five to eighty five. Families, school parties, scouts, guides and ramblers. Wearing plimsols or just bare feet, shorts or bathing costumes, many with rucksacks. A special event is about to take place; a walk across the sands of Morecambe Bay the eleven miles to Kents Bank just west of Grange-over-Sands. Looking north across the bay, the shimmering white dots set on the verdant Grange hillside seem much closer than the eight miles as-the-crow-flies. Behind Grange, the range of Lakeland hills stand as a majestic back drop. An atmosphere of excitement builds amongst the several hundred strong crowd, who become more restless as the official starting time of eleven-thirty passes.

Suddenly the broadly smiling figure of Ced arrives carrying his trusted ash stick, wearing a clean white shirt, jeans and trainers and a small green rucksack. Many recognise him immediately and crowd round. Others follow. Ced, standing on high ground, calls them to attention and addresses the hushed crowd like a prophet. Remarking on the fine weather he jokes that he hasn't lost anybody on the sands yet and tells everyone to keep behind the guide, reminding them that this isn't a race but will take over *four* hours. He evidently loves this part of his job and guides over a dozen such walks each year between May and September.

Ced first takes off and packs his shirt then leads off across the Hest Bank salt-marsh with the multitude filing behind him in a chattering carnival-like procession.

Many of the kids are eager to keep up front with the guide and ask him when they'll find some quicksand to get stuck in and 'How far is it to the water crossing?' We make our way happily into the bay across the smooth damp sand. It feels wonderful to be walking barefoot on this velvet ground but we soon encounter hard ribbed sand which is not so comfortable. This regular pattern of ridges will have been set at right angles to the direction of the last tide's ebb which sculpted them. Just like wind does to a sand dune. The line of walkers now stretches out like elastic behind Ced as the midday sun beats pleasantly on my back but stings the calves of my legs after a while—the sands seem to intensify the sun's rays.

Children at the front run on as they catch sight of the first stretch of water but Ced calls them back. This is the river Keer, flowing out from Carnforth and today running very shallow as it hasn't rained for two weeks. Ced stops before the water to gather up his flock. Declaring the channel safe he allows the kids to race each other into the water and they splash joyfully into the luke-warm stream. On the other side our guide calls a welcome ten minute break for stragglers to catch up while the children enjoy the water to the full.

Our party sets off again, now heading for Jenny Brown's Point, a limestone rock outcrop on the Silverdale shore. Suddenly we come to a brack—a break away in the sand—leading down to a deep dyke containing glassy wet sand. Ced halts the crowd and goes down to probe the glistening surface with his ash stick, ordering us to spread out so we don't follow in one another's tracks which might dangerously soften the sand. As we hurriedly cross, the sand shifts curiously and alarmingly like jelly under bare feet, squeezing sensuously between my toes. The adults look worried but the kids squeal delightedly at the experience. All of us safely climb the other side and after another half hour's walking we reach our half way mark—Jenny Brown's Point—for lunch. Most of the boys are, however, more interested in the pool of liquid mud they've discovered just below the rocks and enthusiastically compete with each other to see who can submerge himself most completely in imitation quicksand. Parents look on disdainfully, but Ced is not concerned; he knows there's no real danger in this particular spot.

After twenty minute's rest we climb the rocky outcrop to avoid an area of real quicksand at the shore margin which Ced heeds well, then down the other side onto smooth safe sand again heading for Kents Bank.

Soon we reach within a hundred yards of the highlight of our adventure—the channel of the River Kent. Ced blows his whistle twice and shouts 'Can we have a gather up here?'—a small boy earnestly enquires 'Do you blow your whistle when you want to have your picture taken?' Our guide walks on ahead into the channel, laughing. Probing the river floor with his trusted staff, he decides it's safe and returns to his charge, instructing them to spread out as before for added safety. Children run to be first to thrash screaming through the water. The startling coolness of the Kent contrasts with the warmth of the previous shallow channels. We wade across with water above our knees, balancing against the river's flow, but all safely reach the far side where kids are already happily flinging wet sand at one another and paddling the surface to bury their legs in manufactured quicksand. Ced calls to the children around him and points to a patch of transparent penny-sized objects shining like jewels on the sand. 'They're tiny jellyfish,' Ced tells the crouching youngsters; 'we call them jujubes.'

'Jujubes'

Now, after nearly three hours, comes the last stage of our journey. We head towards Kents Bank, crossing a wide ankle-deep water filled channel which was once the course of the Kent before it shifted shorewards and this oasis again delights the children. Looking to the east, haze-blue Pennine mountains provide an impressive background to the Kent estuary. After another hour's walking the children have quietened but Kents Bank station is now clearly in view five hundred yards ahead. Half a dozen kids at the front suddenly break rank and race each other to a triumphant finish.

Jean and her elder brother, Paul, are waiting on the shore with a stall set out on the back of a small trailer, selling certificates of the crossing plus drinks, sandwiches and Ced's book 'Sand Pilot' (which I can recommend). Weary but happy walkers thank the guide and clean themselves and their offspring in the clear rock pools then sit along the ramp leading to the station waiting for the next train and their coaches. For all it's an experience they'll never forget. Many will return to do the crossing in future years and discover that no two walks are ever quite the same.

I walk with Ced the fifteen minutes along the shore beside the railway track to Guide's Farm where Olive is preparing a marvellous spread of salad for tea. We eat out on the front lawn. Like a childhood remembered summer's afternoon.

The sun mellows and the time soon comes for me to catch the little diesel pay-train all the way round the bay, to my starting point. Having less than ten minutes to get back to Kents Bank station I hurriedly swallow the last cheese sandwich and bid farewell to the Robinsons, then take a different route back to the station. This time walking the other side of the track along the triangle base of the butter-cup-and-daisy fields of Guide's farm, through the hand smoothed rust iron gate at the end then up and down the limestone wall flanked footpath. A warm scent of wild garlic drifts up from the unkempt undergrowth as I climb over the railings, down the embankment, through an unofficial track between nettles and brambles to the railway line. Hearing the train's whistle in the distance I start to run along the rust brown sleepers the three hundred yards to the station; leaping onto the end of the platform just as the two-carriage train squeaks to a halt. Sweating and tired, I drop into a window seat on the left hand side to wave happily to the Robinson's as the train clatters past Guide's Farm two minutes later, with the contentment of a day lived to the full.

AUTUMN COCKLING

By Autumn the following year—called 'the back end' by local fisherfolk—Guide's Farm was like a second home and I regarded the Robinsons as a second family. Indeed Ced had once touchingly remarked 'welcome home' with a genuine smile when answering the door to me.

Jean was now married to Chris Jackson, a farmer's son, from Claughton near Lancaster and they were living in the converted attic of Guide's Farm. She had gently but firmly coaxed me into doing her wedding photos, though I had never been to a wedding in my life, let alone photographed one. But on the day, despite wind and rain, my pictures turned out quite well. Ced and Olive seemed pleased with Jean's choice of partner. Chris was happy to help out around Guide's Farm and regularly went out on the sands to help Ced fishing. Jean wasn't too concerned about Chris taking over her assistant's role as she was well occupied in looking after the half dozen horses and ponies on the farm which she took pony trekking in the warmer months, to earn some extra cash.

On one of my, by now, regular visits to the farm, Jean informed me of her latest theory; 'The reason we're all crackers,' she declared triumphantly 'is the lead in our pipes!' I was saddened to hear that Eva had suffered a heart attack and had been in hospital, but was now recovering well.

Ced gave me a vivid account of the day Mrs. Williams—an elderly friend who typed his manuscripts—phoned up to inform him that the *Vietnamese Ambassador* would be visiting him that afternoon. He thanked her, no doubt wondering whether or not senility had set in overnight. Guide's Farm had at the time been literally turned upside down as the family were decorating. At two o'clock prompt, a long black limousine drew up in front of Guide's Farm and a short, smartly dressed oriental gentleman stepped out, flanked by his entourage. Ced, unaware of this opened the door with brush in hand, wearing a pair of tattered paint spattered jeans, as the knocker sounded and was promptly kissed on both unshaven cheeks by the smiling diplomat. Chris looked on amused, sporting safety pins in place of a broken fly zip. Poor Olive didn't know what to say, but the visitor made it clear that he quite understood and stayed for tea, anyway.

I looked out through the living room window which gave a magnificent view of the bay on this unusually clear day; from just beyond Jenny Brown's Point, round to Holme Island. Olive came in to say hello to me, and told Ced that she had just had an order for two bags of cockles but there were none to sell. Ced and Chris agreed to go out on the sands the same day to collect some, and looking at his tide tables Ced declared that they should leave at two-thirty. I eagerly asked to come along and take some pictures.

So we set off for the sands once more, on a crisply cold, but sunny afternoon, with Chris and myself riding on the trailer. This time however we couldn't use the usual railway crossing as Eva wasn't yet fully fit. We turned instead up the steep hill of Carter Road in first gear, then gently down hill the mile to Kents Bank station. While we waited for the crossing keeper to appear, Chris suddenly remarked 'Oh, no, we've left the cockle baskets behind!' Ced wasn't about to go all the way back and looking around him caught sight of the empty D shaped wire waste paper baskets on the station platform. 'I'm sure they wouldn't mind us borrowing them for a while' said Ced. So Chris swiftly requisitioned two of these splendid items and by the time the keeper appeared, the acquisitions had been stowed carefully out of view. We rumbled down to the glutinous mud of the foreshore, then set course for the cockle beds near the end of Cartmel Wharf; just about as far into the bay as you can go. Ced turned, laughing, 'Watch out for Beeches Bruke!', as we careered into a steep sided channel. I could clearly see the entire arc of the bay from Blackpool Tower beyond Fleetwood, to Heysham, Morecambe to Warton Crag, Silverdale, Arnside Knot and then round past Grange to Piel Island and the distant silhouette of the massive ship yard cranes at Barrow. Familiar places seen from an unfamiliar and ever-shifting viewpoint.

We headed steadily towards Heysham, passing the grassed limestone outcrop of Humphrey Head, said to be the place where the last wild wolf in England was shot. After another quarter of an hour of brisk progress, Heysham didn't seem as close as I would expect; distances viewed across the bay are deceptive. Another fifteen minutes passed, then, without warning we stopped on an area of sand which at first seemed to be like any other. But Ced knew he had arrived at the cockle beds. We unloaded out apparatus and Ced pointed to tiny brown filaments sprouting from the sands–'Cockles are rank here!' he declared. Rank means plentiful in the Flookburgh dialect, also whee-at means small or immature cockles, I learned.

Ced hauled the jumbo across the sand and set to work. This implement, thought to be unique to the Flookburgh fisherfolk, is a wooden plank about one foot by four, attached to a pair of handles at waist height by two metal or wood uprights. The plank is rocked to and fro on the sands to soften them, causing the cockles buried an inch or so below the surface to float upwards into view. The cockles *can* then be flicked into a net using a three pronged hand fork called a cramb. Some Flookburgh men are able to pick up a hundred or more cockles a minute by this method *but* this day, Chris used a short handled rake to gather them while Ced energetically rocked the jumbo. Pulling it back after every five or six rocks to prepare a strip of sand for Chris to work on. The expression, 'rocking the jumbo' belies the back breaking effort involved, especially when the sand is relatively dry and hard, as I found when Ced let me have a go. Chris raked the cockles into a riddle and poured them into the railway receptacles which seemed to have just the right sized mesh for the job, then washed and filled the shellfish into plastic sacks.

The sun balanced on the horizon as the last load of cockles was added to top up the second bag, though it had only just turned five-thirty. 'That's enough for one day,' beamed Ced, his normally ruddy face appearing even redder in the magenta afterglow. Looking at Ced in the twilight on the lonely bay, I suddenly felt a warm affection for this friendly man, with his now-luminescent oilskin bound tightly at the waist by a length of string.

Turning round I discovered a full moon sitting on the Pennine hills to the east, as if displaced, see-saw like, in perfect opposition to the setting sun. Using an upturned bucket on top of one jumbo handle as a makeshift tripod—Ced's idea—I photographed the moonlit bay. An unforgettable sight. It seemed strangely appropriate; without the moon there would be no tide and without the tide's ebb and flow, this unique way of life would not exist.

As purple dusk rapidly gathered itself in around us, a string of orange street lights could be seen, stretching round the coast road from Heysham to Carnforth. To the north, a tiny cluster of pin points which was Flookburgh and just east of this, an array of jewelled points stacked on the Grange hillside. Ced steered for this beacon on the homeward journey, passing Humphrey Head once more, which this time loomed as a menacing black shadow. Soon we thankfully reached the gates of Kents Bank crossing but had to wait, stranded, for a cold ten minutes before the keeper emerged, to free us.

Olive was relieved when we at last returned, by the light of the moon, after four hours away. She soon gave us a delicious meal of roast chicken and Jean's apple pie to finish, accompanied by last years home made damson wine—a potent brew. Thereafter, Ced, Jean and Olive soon yielded to sleep in front of the eternal flames at the heart of Guide's Farm.

IDYL

Northwards from Heysham

Previous page – Morning at Arnside

Humphrey Head, seen from Silverdale

Overleaf – The Shadow of Holme Island to the right, from New Barns

Mussel beds at Morecambe

Overleaf – A few hundred yards out from Sandylands , Morecambe

THE PHOTOGRAPHS

I would firstly like to say that all the photographs in this book are 'guaranteed free from artificial colouring' which means that no special effect filters have been used–the colours you see are the colours of nature. This is important to me. Photography is unique in allowing us to honestly record the subtle effects of light the way they are, and show these to others, saying, 'aren't those colours, tones, textures, shapes, wonderful?' This approach allows you plenty of scope for real self expression by the choice of subject, viewpoint, framing, lighting, and exposure. I believe that the film used is more important than the camera, and go to some trouble to find batches of film which have a neutral colour balance. This I do by buying one roll and quickly testing it against a colour chart then, if the batch is a good one, I go back and buy 20 or 30 rolls of the same. The reality is that rolls of fresh film from even the *top* manufacturers, vary enormously in colour balance between batches and a change in speed equivalent to one stop is not unusual, when changing from one batch to another of the same film. Incidentally, the colour balance of films, changes with age, so you may find some films reach a neutral balance one, or even two years after they are bought.

You may like to know that my camera equipment has now been trimmed down to a Pentax 6×7 body with prism finder, 55, 90 and 165 mm lenses and a Weston meter-and we're all very happy together. Finally, if you use colour transparency film, as I do (the standard for publication), a hand–held incident light meter is really the best way of getting the exposure right, i.e. within half a stop.

PAGE	LIGHT	FILM	CAMERA	LENS
1	Sun	Kodachrome 64	Olympus 35RC	42 mm
2	Sun	Kodachrome 64	Nikon FE	35 mm
9	Hazy Morning Sun	Kodachrome 64	Olympus 35RC	42 mm
10	Stormy sky	Kodachrome 64	Olympus 35RC	42 mm
12	Sun	Kodachrome 25	Olympus OM2	24 mm
13	Overcast	Kodachrome 64	Nikon FE	24 mm
14	Dusk	Kodachrome 64	Olympus 35RC	42 mm
16T	Hazy sun	Kodachrome 25	Olympus OM2	24 mm
16B	Sun	Kodachrome 64	Olympus 35RC	42 mm
17	Sun	Kodachrome 64	Nikon FE	35 mm
18	Sun	Agfachrome R100s	Pentax 67	55 mm
20	Overcast	Kodachrome 64	Nikon FE	35 mm
21	After sundown	Ektachrome 200	Pentax 67	55 mm
23	Sun	Agfachrome R100s	Pentax 67	90 mm
25	Sun	Agfachrome R100s	Pentax 67	90 mm
27	Sun	Kodachrome 64	Nikon FE	35 mm
28	Hazy sun	Kodachrome 64	Nikon FE	24 mm
29	Overcast	Kodachrome 64	Nikon FE	35 mm
31	Overcast	Agfachrome R100s	Pentax 67	165 mm
32	Overcast	Ektachrome 200	Nikon FE	35 mm
33	Overcast	Ektachrome 200	Nikon FE	24 mm
34 L	Overcast	Ektachrome 200	Nikon FE	24 mm
34R	Overcast	Ektachrome 299	Nikon FE	24 mm
35T	Overcast	Ektachrome 200	Nikon FE	35 mm
35B	Overcat	Ektachrome 200	Nikon FE	24 mm
36	Hazy sun	Agfachrome CT18	Pentax 67	55 mm
38	Hazy sun	Kodachrome 64	Nikon FE	50 mm

PAGE	LIGHT	FILM	CAMERA	LENS
39	Hazy sun	Kodachrome 64	Nikon FE	35 mm
40	Hazy sun	Kodachrome 64	Nikon FE	35 mm
42	Electronic Flash	Kodachrome 64	Nikon FE	35 mm
43	Sun	Kodachrome 64	Nikon FE	24 mm
44	Sun	Kodachrome 64	Nikon FE	200 mm
45L	Room light	Kodachrome 64	Nikon FE	35 mm
45R	Room light	Ektachrome 200	Hasselblad ELM	80 mm
47	Window light	Agfachrome R100s	Pentax 67	90 mm
48	Overcast	Kodachrome 64	Nikon FE	35 mm
49	Overcast	Kodachrome 64	Nikon FE	35 mm
50	Overcast	Kodachrome 64	Nikon FE	35 mm
51	Hazy sun	Kodachrome 64	Nikon FE	35 mm
52	Overcast	Ektachrome 200	Nikon FE	50 mm
53	Overcast	Kodachrome 64	Nikon FE	35 mm
54	Sun	Kodachrome 64	Nikon FE	35 mm
57	Sun	Agfachrome R100s	Pentax 67	165 mm
58	Sun	Agfachrome R100s	Pentax 67	165 mm
60	Sun	Agfachrome R100s	Pentax 67	90 mm
62	Sun	Agfachrome R100s	Pentax 67	165 mm
64	Sun	Agfachrome R100s	Pentax 67	90 mm
65T	Sun	Agfachrome R100s	Pentax 67	90 mm
65B	Shade	Agfachrome R100s	Pentax 67	165 mm
66	Sun	Kodachrome 64	Olympus OM2	35 mm
67T	Sun	Agfachrome R100s	Penax 67	55 mm
67B	Sun	Agfachrome R100s	Pentax 67	55 mm
68	Sun	Kodachrome 64	Nikon FE	35 mm
69T	Sun	Kodachrome 64	Nikon FE	35 mm
69B	Sun	Kodachrome 64	Nikon FE	35 mm
70T	Sun	Kodachrome 64	Olympus 35RC	42 mm
70B	Sun	Ektachrome 64	Hasselblad ELM	80 mm
71T	Sun	Agfachrome R100s	Pentax 67	55 mm
71B	Sun	Agfachrome R100s	Pentax 67	90 mm
72	Sun	Agfachrome R100s	Pentax 67	90 mm
73T	Sun	Kodachrome 64	Nikon FE	35 mm
73B	Sun	Agfachrome R100s	Pentax 67	55 mm
74	Sun	Agfachrome R100s	Pentax 67	55 mm
77	Sun	Agfachrome R100s	Pentax 67	55 mm
78	Sun	Agfachrome R100s	Pentax 67	55 mm
79	Low sun	Agfachrome R100s	Pentax 67	55 mm
80	Low sun	Agfachrome R100s	Pentax 67	55 mm
81	Low sun	Ektachrome 200	Pentax 67	55 mm
82	After sundown	Ektachrome 200	Pentax 67	90 mm
83	Dusk	Agfachrome R100s	Pentax 67	90 mm
84	Hazy Morning Sun	Kodachrome 64	Olympus 35RC	42 mm
86	After sundown	Kodachrome 64	Nikon FE	200 mm
87	Sunset	Kodachrome 64	Olympus 35RC	42 mm
88	After sundown	Kodachrome 64	Olympus 35RC	42 mm
90	Sunset	Kodachrome 25	Olympus OM2	150 mm
92	Sunset	Kodachrome 25	Olympus OM2	24 mm
96T	Overcast	Agfachrome R100s	Hasselblad ELM	80 mm
96B	Overcast	Ektachrome 200	Nikon FE	35 mm

A special day for the pupils from Allithwaite School. Matthew Kelly came to present a 'Madabout' programme on the bay, featuring the children with Ced, who took them all out on his tractor and trailer.